BIODIVERSITY

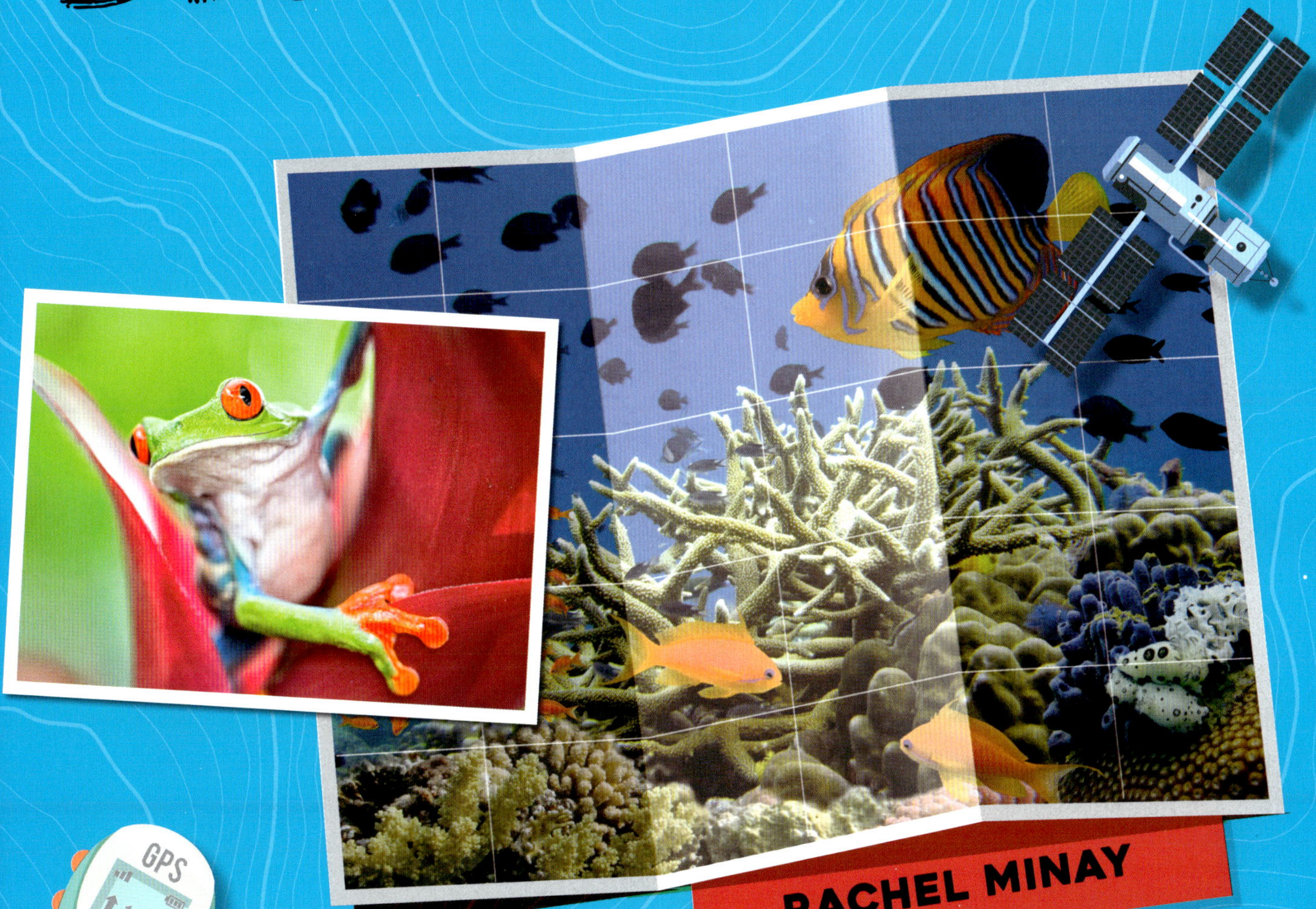

RACHEL MINAY

W FRANKLIN WATTS
LONDON • SYDNEY

Franklin Watts

First published in Great Britain in 2021 by the Watts Publishing Group

Copyright © the Watts Publishing Group 2021

 Produced for Franklin Watts by White-Thomson Publishing Ltd
www.wtpub.co.uk

All rights reserved.

Editor: Rachel Minay
Designer: Clare Nicholas
Series designer: Rocket Design (East Anglia) Ltd

HB ISBN: 978 1 4451 7367 2
PB ISBN: 978 1 4451 7368 9

The publisher would like to thank the following for permission to reproduce their pictures:
Getty : webguzs 10(b), serpeblu 11(b), Dimitrios Stefanidis 14(t); NASA: 24–25; Shutterstock: Dirk Ercken cover (inset), Vlad61 cover (main), Pixel-joy 4, Goran Bogicevic 5(b), Colette3 5(c), Emre Terim/Julian Baker 5(t), Roman Khomlyak 7, Quick Shot 7(b), Gabriel Pfister 7(t), Jag_cz 8, Chainarong Phrammanee 9(b), Jones & Shimlock / Jaynes Gallery / DanitaDelimont.com 9(t), Longjourneys 10(c), Dr Ajay Kumar Singh 10(t), Olha1981 11(t), Jess Kraft 13(t), Don Landwehrle 15, Ondrej Prosicky 16(bl), VectorMine 16(br), Dudarev Mikhail 16(t), Craig139 17(b), Angela N Perryman 17(t), J.K. York 18(b), colin robert varndell 18(c), Menno Schaefer 18(t), David G Hayes 19(b), Jukka Jantunen 20(b), Robyn Butler 20(t), Houshmand Rabbani 21(b), Stanislav Fosenbauer 21(t), Ilgonisf 22(b), guentermanaus 22(t), Valentin Valkov 23, K.Chuansakul 23(b), Artush 26(b), Jono Photography 26(c), Joseph Sohm 27(b), Barnes Ian 27(t), blueeyes 28(b), Chase Dekker 29(b), David Osborn 29(c), Bildagentur Zoonar GmbH 29(t).

Design elements by Shutterstock.

Map illustrations: Julian Baker: 8–9, 12–13, 16–17, 20–21, 28–29.

Every effort has been made to clear copyright. Should there be any inadvertent omission, please apply to the publisher for rectification.

The website addresses (URLs) included in this book were valid at the time of going to press. However, it is possible that contents or addresses may have changed since the publication of this book. No responsibility for any such changes can be accepted by either the author or the publisher.

All facts and statistics were correct at the time of press.

Printed in Dubai

Franklin Watts
An imprint of
Hachette Children's Group,
Part of the Watts Publishing Group
Carmelite House
50 Victoria Embankment
London EC4Y 0DZ

An Hachette UK Company
www.hachettechildrens.co.uk

CONTENTS

What is biodiversity? 4
Why do we need biodiversity? 6
📍 **Mapping the Coral Triangle** 8
Evolution and extinction 10
📍 **Mapping the Galápagos Islands** 12
Ecosystems 14
📍 **Mapping Madagascar** 16
Invasive species 18
📍 **Mapping Australia** 20
Biodiversity under threat 22
📍 **Mapping the Amazon Rainforest** 24
Protecting biodiversity 26
📍 **Mapping North America** 28
Glossary 30
Further information 31
Index 32

WHAT IS BIODIVERSITY?

Biodiversity means the variety of plant and animal life in an area. It is important for many reasons, including for food, health and raw materials. Biodiversity is vital to life on Earth – now and in the future.

Biodiversity is not about the number of a few species, but about the variety of different species.

LEVELS OF BIODIVERSITY

There are three levels of biodiversity:

1. **Genetic diversity** is all the different genes within a species. Genes are the parts of living cells that control which characteristics are passed on from parents.
2. **Species diversity** is all the different kinds of plants and animals, and variations within them.
3. **Ecosystem diversity** is all the different habitats on the planet.

DIFFERENT ECOSYSTEMS

An ecosystem is the living things in an area and how they affect each other and their environment. Some ecosystems have more biodiversity than others – for example the frozen polar regions are not very biodiverse, but a tropical rainforest has an amazing variety of plants and animals.

HUMAN IMPACT

We rely on biodiversity for food, clean air and more, but it is seriously under threat. While this is sometimes due to natural causes, such as earthquakes, the greatest threat is human activity, such as the clearing of habitats to grow crops or build houses, pollution and climate change.

BIODIVERSITY HOTSPOTS

A biodiversity hotspot is a place with a high percentage of plant life found nowhere else, but which has lost 70 per cent or more of its original vegetation. This means biodiversity hotspots are very important, but also deeply threatened. However, international organisations and local groups are working to protect them.

This map shows the world's biodiversity hotspots.

① ATLANTIC FOREST

South America's eastern coast was once covered by over 1 million square km of the Atlantic Forest – now, just 7 per cent remains.

② MEDITERRANEAN

Tourism has taken its toll on the beautiful Mediterranean, leading to habitat loss, exploitation of marine life and pollution.

③ WESTERN GHATS

The Western Ghats, a mountain range in India, are home to 10 per cent of the world's tigers. Once common in Asia, habitat loss means tigers have lost a massive 93 per cent of their range over the last century.

WHY DO WE NEED BIODIVERSITY?

One way to think of biodiversity is as a shield that protects each of the species that make it up – including humans. So how does it help us?

WE NEED BIODIVERSITY FOR:

FOOD
Plants, livestock, birds and fish
Potential future food
Pollinators and pest controllers

HEALTH
Nutrition from a mix of foods helps us fight disease
Medicines
Potential medicines

HEALTHY PLANET
Clean air
Clean water
Healthy soil

RAW MATERIALS
Wood
Biofuels
Fibres to make clothes

STRONG ECOSYSTEMS
To better cope with changes

ETHICAL REASONS
Our responsibility to look after the planet

BEAUTY OF NATURE
Can improve our physical and mental health
Can make us feel calmer or more creative

Many species play a vital role in the food we eat, including ones that pollinate crops or eat pests that would damage them.

FACT

Three-quarters of wild flowering plants and about a third of the world's food crops depend on pollination.

Biodiverse ecosystems are very useful for medicines. About 70 per cent of plants with cancer-fighting properties are found in rainforests. Scientists also worry that some plants may go extinct before we have discovered if they could be used to fight disease in the future.

We live on a beautiful planet, but humans are the species that cause it the most damage. Many people think it is our duty to protect biodiversity and the wonder of the natural world.

MAPPING THE CORAL TRIANGLE

The most biodiverse marine area on Earth is the Coral Triangle in Southeast Asia.

CRUCIAL CORAL

Coral reefs provide food and shelter for marine life. Local people also rely on them for food, as well as for income from fishing and tourism. Reefs can protect coasts from strong currents and waves. They are also part of a healthy planet, cleaning water and helping to control levels of carbon dioxide in the water and the air. However, reefs are under threat from climate change. Warmer seas lead to coral 'bleaching' – when this happens, the coral begins to starve.

The Coral Triangle covers 6 million square km and spans six countries.

MALAYSIA

PHILIPPINES

INDONESIA

TIMOR LESTE

CORAL TRIANGLE

Indian Ocean

Coral reefs attract tourists. This is good for the economy, but tourism needs to be sustainable to reduce its impact on the marine environment.

FACT

A huge 76 per cent of the world's 798 coral species can be found here.

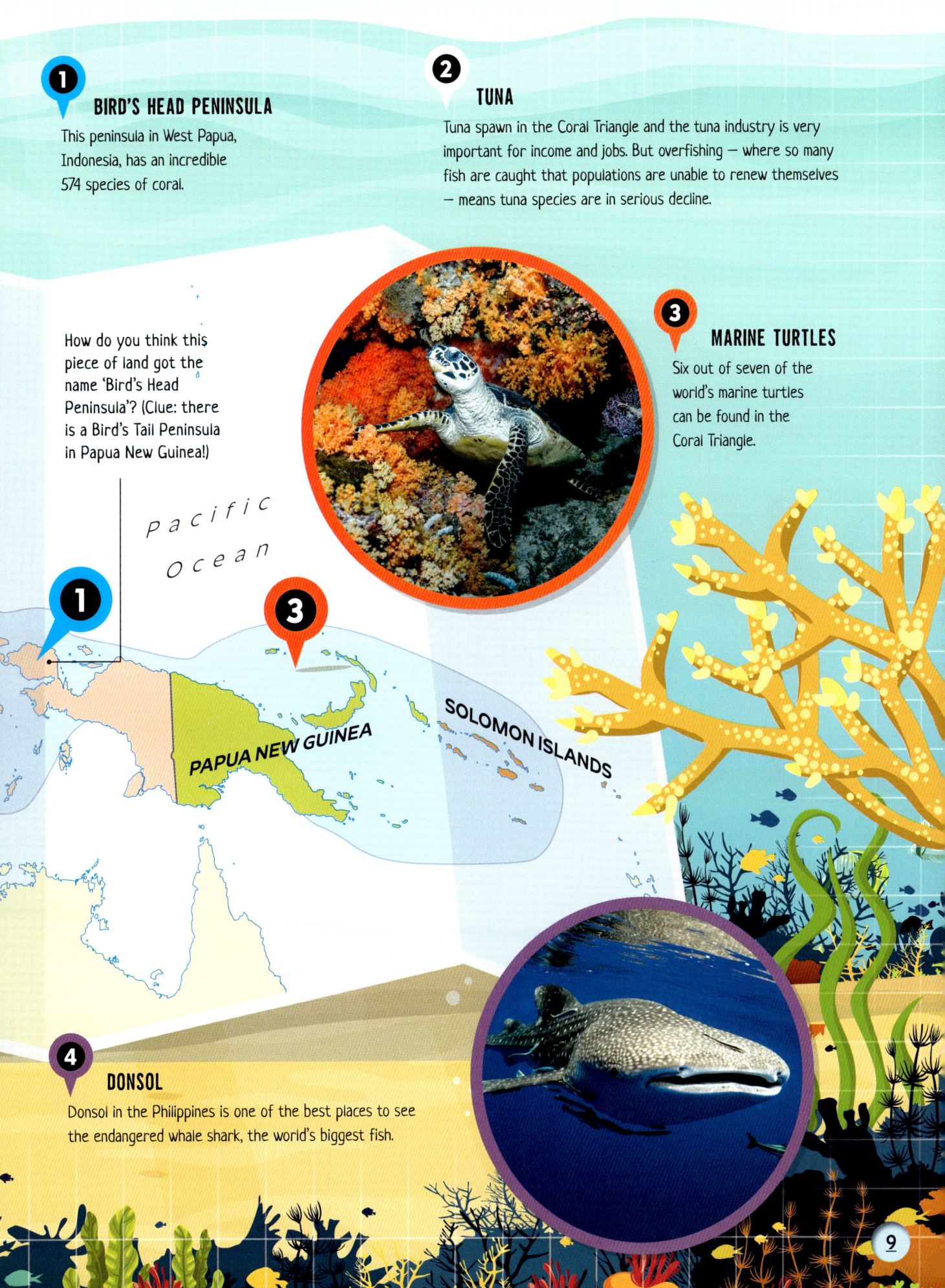

1 BIRD'S HEAD PENINSULA
This peninsula in West Papua, Indonesia, has an incredible 574 species of coral.

2 TUNA
Tuna spawn in the Coral Triangle and the tuna industry is very important for income and jobs. But overfishing — where so many fish are caught that populations are unable to renew themselves — means tuna species are in serious decline.

How do you think this piece of land got the name 'Bird's Head Peninsula'? (Clue: there is a Bird's Tail Peninsula in Papua New Guinea!)

3 MARINE TURTLES
Six out of seven of the world's marine turtles can be found in the Coral Triangle.

4 DONSOL
Donsol in the Philippines is one of the best places to see the endangered whale shark, the world's biggest fish.

EVOLUTION AND EXTINCTION

Evolution is the way living things gradually change over time. Earth's biodiversity is the result of 4 billion years of evolution.

EVOLUTION

In 1859, the naturalist Charles Darwin wrote about evolution and something he called 'natural selection'. He said species with characteristics that were better adapted for survival were more likely to reproduce and pass these characteristics on to their offspring. Over time, this leads to gradual changes in a species and eventually to new species.

Cheetahs have evolved to have a streamlined shape, powerful legs and a camouflaged coat — making them speedy and stealthy hunters.

Sea lions have evolved with a smooth shape and powerful muscles to move swiftly through the water. Blubber, or fat, underneath the skin helps keep them warm.

A hummingbird has a long, narrow beak to feed on nectar from flowers. Hummingbirds are adapted to hover, and fly backwards and upside-down!

EXTINCTION

Some species have always evolved more successfully than others, but human activity means thousands of species are endangered – at risk of extinction. If a species is extinct, there are no more of that species anywhere in the world.

MASS EXTINCTIONS

There have been five mass extinctions in Earth's history, all of which were due to natural causes, such as volcanic eruptions or ice ages. Many people believe we're entering a sixth mass extinction – caused by humans.

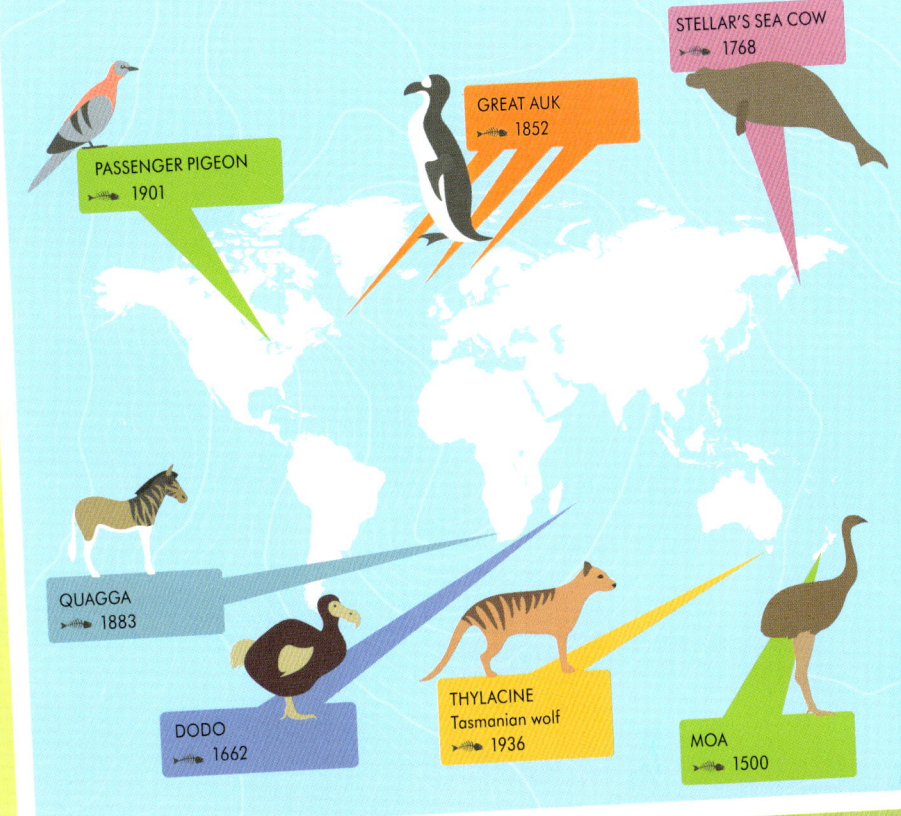

MAP MASTERS

Maps can show us a wide range of things and they can be simple or very detailed. This map shows information about some extinct animals in an easy-to-understand way.

PASSENGER PIGEON 1901
GREAT AUK 1852
STELLAR'S SEA COW 1768
QUAGGA 1883
DODO 1662
THYLACINE Tasmanian wolf 1936
MOA 1500

An asteroid impact is thought to have caused the fifth mass extinction, 66 million years ago. Three-quarters of all the species on Earth were wiped out, including the dinosaurs.

MAPPING THE GALÁPAGOS ISLANDS

Darwin wrote about evolution after a trip to one of the most biodiverse places on the planet – the Galápagos Islands.

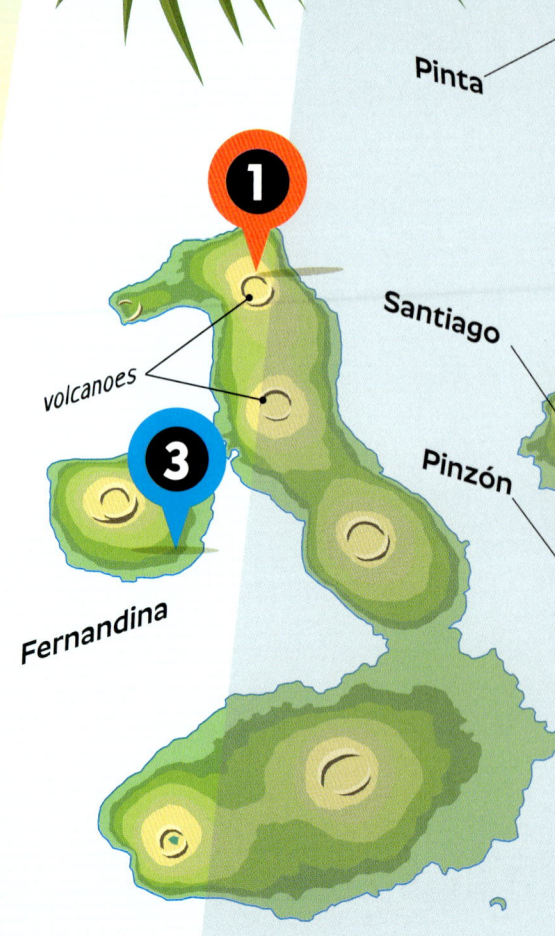

MAP MASTERS

The Galápagos are in the Pacific Ocean, west of Ecuador. In 1831 a ship called HMS Beagle set out to thoroughly map the area for sailors. The captain thought it would be useful to have a naturalist on board – this was Darwin.

WHY ARE ISLANDS SPECIAL?

Islands can be small, but they make a big contribution to biodiversity! Species can evolve in unusual ways when they are isolated from other land and confined to a small area. This means islands are often home to endemic species – ones that are found nowhere else on Earth.

FACT

An astonishing 97 per cent of the reptiles and land mammals, 80 per cent of the land birds, and more than 30 per cent of the plants in the Galápagos are endemic.

Marchena

Genovesa

Pacific Ocean

Two unique Galápagos species are the marine iguana and the flightless cormorant. The iguana is the only lizard that has evolved to feed in the sea, while the cormorant can swim strongly, but has lost the ability to fly.

Baltra

Santa Cruz

Santa Fé

San Cristóbal

Floreana

Española

GALÁPAGOS ISLANDS

AMAZING ADAPATIONS

An island species might evolve to be much bigger or smaller than the same animal on the mainland, depending on food sources or predators. Without a top predator, an island species might grow much larger as it doesn't need to hide. However, if food is in short supply, small species are more likely to survive and reproduce. A lack of predators can also mean some birds become flightless over time, as they don't need to fly to escape danger.

1 VOLCANIC ISLANDS
Formed by volcanic action, the Galápagos are made up of 13 major and 7 smaller islands.

2 SPECIES ARRIVAL
When the islands were formed millions of years ago, they were without plant or animal life. So how did the unique species get here? The answers are by air or by sea, either swimming or drifting on 'rafts' of vegetation.

3 GIANT TORTOISE
Darwin first saw giant tortoises on Chatham Island (now San Cristóbal). At the time, the tortoises were seen as food and some species became extinct. One species feared to be extinct was the Fernandina Island giant tortoise, as it was last seen in 1906 — however, one elderly female was found in 2019.

ECOSYSTEMS

Earth is home to a range of ecosystems, from the smallest rock pool to a vast desert. An ecosystem is made up of living things, as well as the non-living parts of the environment, such as water and soil. More biodiversity means a stronger ecosystem.

Freshwater ecosystems are the least common — less than 2 per cent cover Earth's surface.

Ocean ecosystems cover more than 70 per cent of the surface.

The biggest ecosystem on Earth is the planet itself.

FOOD CHAINS AND WEBS

All the living things in an ecosystem rely on each other and their environment to live and reproduce. Plants rely on soil, water and the Sun. Animals rely on plants and other animals. This can be shown through simple food chains (for example **plant → rabbit → hawk**) or more complex food webs.

A food web is just a number of food chains linked in the same ecosystem. For example, this web shows
plant → rabbit → hawk
but also
plant → mouse → snake → hawk
and others.

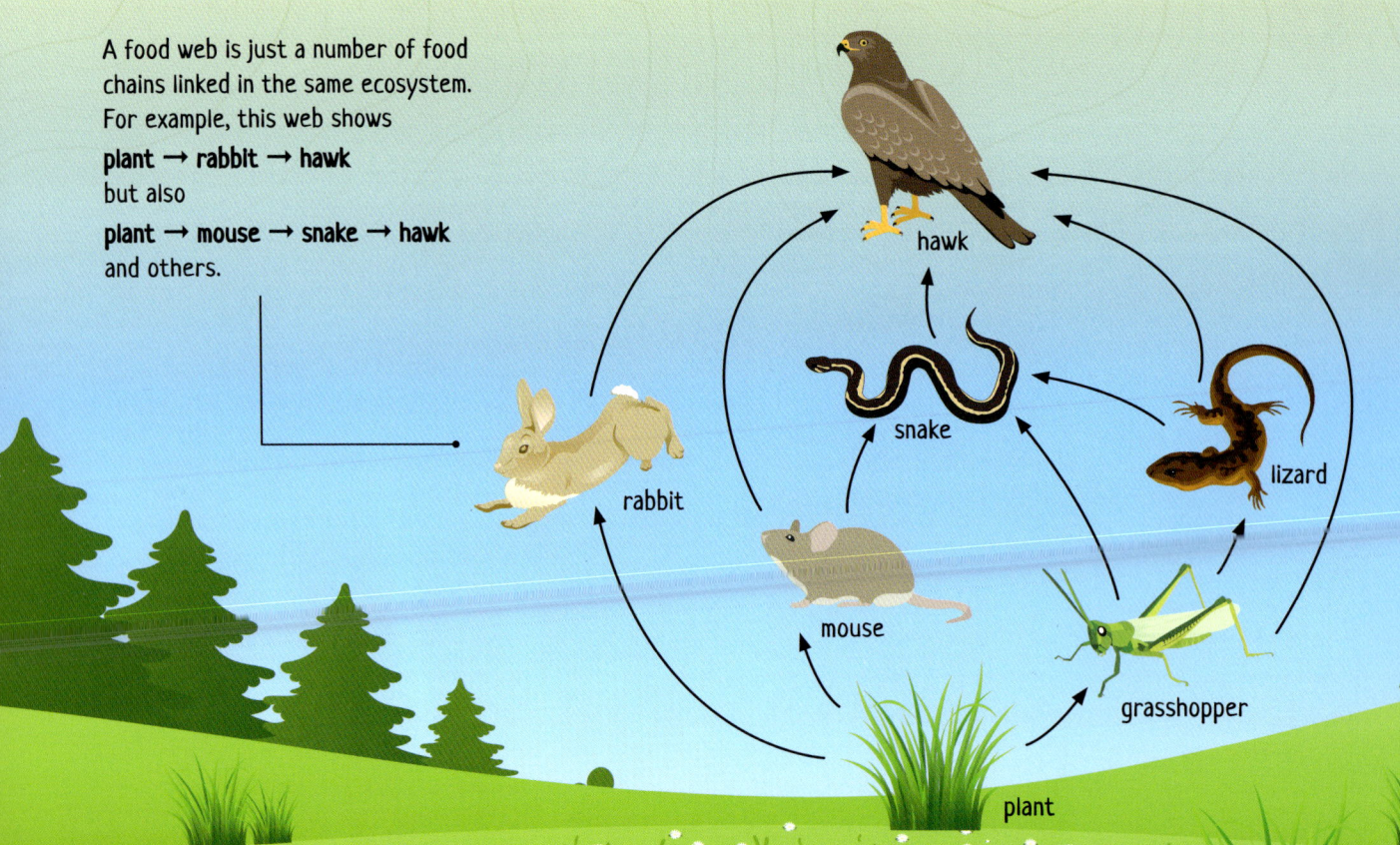

CHANGES

Ecosystems are very sensitive to change. Living things can be affected by new predators, competition from other species, new diseases and how much food is available. Changes to non-living parts include a change in temperature or moisture level.

Look again at the picture of a food web. Imagine the grasshopper population goes down, perhaps due to a new disease. The hawk can still eat rabbits and mice, but the lizard population would go down as grasshoppers are its main food source. The snake would be affected too, as there are now fewer grasshoppers and also fewer lizards. Now imagine there is a severe drought and all the plants die – this would affect the entire web right up to the hawk, the apex (top) predator.

HOW CAN BIODIVERSITY HELP?

A species that relies on just one other species to survive is very vulnerable. Higher biodiversity in an ecosystem means fewer species depend on just one other, so biodiverse ecosystems can cope better with changes.

Think again about the food web and the example of severe drought. If some of the plants were drought-tolerant species, they would survive and provide a food source for the animals until other plants recovered.

An indicator is a species that tells scientists about the health of an ecosystem. Polar bears, which are vulnerable because of habitat loss caused by climate change, are an indicator of Arctic ecosystem health.

MAPPING MADAGASCAR

Madagascar is so unique, some people call it the eighth continent! This biodiverse island is home to a wide range of ecosystems.

 1 LOWLAND FOREST
Between 80 and 90 per cent of the plants and animals in this rich rainforest are endemic, including the critically endangered Indri lemur.

2 SUBHUMID FOREST
This was once home to the now-extinct 'elephant bird', a flightless bird that stood 3 m tall!

 3 DRY DECIDUOUS FOREST
Many of Madagascar's birds can be found in the dry deciduous forests, including the crested coua.

MAP MASTERS

These maps show 200 million years on Earth. Madagascar was once landlocked as part of the supercontinent Pangaea. Over time, the continents broke up, leaving Madagascar to evolve as a unique island.

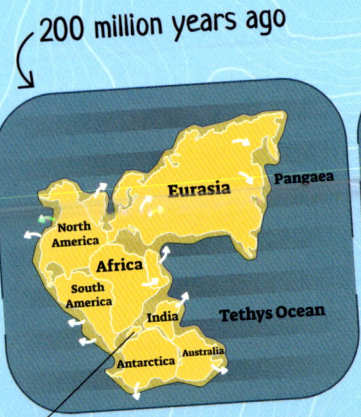
200 million years ago

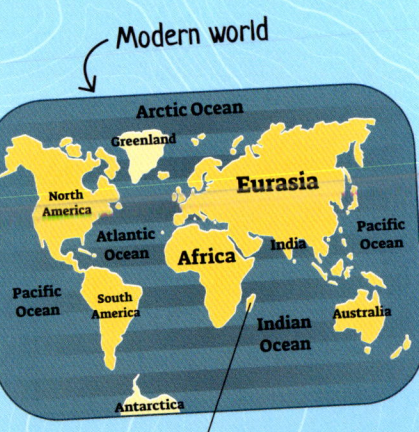
Modern world

FACT
Madagascar is home to 250,000 species.

Legend:
- Subhumid forest
- Spiny thicket
- Succulent woodland
- Dry deciduous forest
- Lowland forest
- Mangroves

This map shows the rich variety of ecoregions (areas with similar ecosystems) in Madagascar.

Madagascar is best known for lemurs — it is the only place they can be found in the wild. Habitat loss due to deforestation means nearly all of the over 100 species of lemur are rare, vulnerable or endangered.

MADAGASCAR: AFRICA

4 SUCCULENT WOODLAND
This area includes the Avenue of the Baobabs, a spectacular group of an endemic yet endangered species of tree.

5 SPINY THICKET
The spiny thicket in the south-west is very dry, with spiny shrubs and trees.

6 MANGROVE
Mangroves, trees that grow in salty coastal swamps, are important for wildlife.

7 CORAL REEF
Madagascar has 1,000 km of coral reef.

INVASIVE SPECIES

Invasive species can upset the balance and biodiversity of an ecosystem. These are non-native animals or plants that are introduced – accidentally or on purpose – and spread in a way that causes damage.

CAUSING PROBLEMS

Introducing a species does not always make it invasive – many crops, for example, are grown in areas they did not come from originally. Something becomes invasive when it starts to take over an ecosystem, causing real problems for the species already living there.

Red squirrels were once common in the UK, but numbers have plummeted following the introduction of grey squirrels in the 1870s.

Grey squirrels compete more successfully for food and habitat, and also carry a disease that does not affect them but kills red squirrels.

Unchecked, the kudzu vine spreads quickly, smothering other plants. Native to Asia, it was introduced to the USA as an ornamental plant. It became a big problem in the southern states, gaining the nickname 'the vine that ate the South'.

HOW DID THEY GET THERE?

Sometimes, people travelling around the world have carried invasive species with them without even realising. For example, rats have spread widely by hitching rides on ships. Other times, people have introduced species on purpose – only to find out later how problematic they are. They can be particularly damaging on islands, where they may have no natural predators and so spread quickly, squeezing out more vulnerable native species.

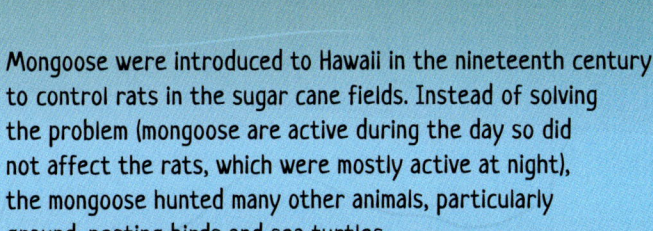

Mongoose were introduced to Hawaii in the nineteenth century to control rats in the sugar cane fields. Instead of solving the problem (mongoose are active during the day so did not affect the rats, which were mostly active at night), the mongoose hunted many other animals, particularly ground-nesting birds and sea turtles.

SOLUTIONS

Solutions include using herbicides on problem plants, and trapping and killing animals. Biological control is using one species to control another. In the 1880s, the cottony-cushion scale insect was destroying the citrus industry in California. Importing its natural predators, ladybirds, solved the problem within two years.

MAPPING AUSTRALIA

Australia's isolation and climate have led to its unique wildlife, including kangaroos, koalas, emus and the platypus – a mammal that lays eggs! Unfortunately, invasive species are a huge problem in this biodiverse country.

There are over 50 invasive animal species in Australia; this map focuses on four of them.

Timor Sea

Western Australia

Perth

Great Australian Bight

AUSTRALIA

1 CANE TOAD

Cane toads were introduced to control a native beetle, but became a much bigger pest. Packed with poison, cane toads kill native species that try to eat them, and they damage habitats. They can cope with a range of conditions and have bred and spread at high speed.

2 RED FOX

Foxes were introduced in the 1800s for hunting, but have become a widespread predator of endemic species.

Many species were introduced to Australia as a result of European colonisation.

4 AUSTRALIAN FERAL CAMEL

Feral species are domestic animals that have gone wild. There are feral cats, goats and pigs in Australia, but did you know that there are also feral camels? Originally imported for transport, they were turned loose and damage both the environment and towns.

3 EUROPEAN RABBIT

Rabbits were brought in as a food source. There are now more than 200 million of these prolific breeders, and overgrazing has a huge effect on local species and the environment.

BIODIVERSITY UNDER THREAT

The problems caused by invasive species are just one threat to Earth's biodiversity. There are various reasons that 1 million plant and animal species are threatened with extinction – but most are due to human activity.

HABITAT LOSS

A major threat to biodiversity is habitat loss – a species will clearly suffer if the place that it depends on for shelter, food and mates is destroyed. Sometimes habitats are destroyed by natural events, but human activities are the main cause. Clearing land for housing, farming, mining and road-building always destroys habitats.

Hundreds of species of plant, animal and insect may be lost each day to deforestation. This directly causes loss of habitats and biodiversity, and extinction.

CLIMATE CRISIS

Another huge issue is the changing climate. Rising temperatures and rising sea levels affect the distribution of species, migration and breeding patterns, all of which can result in populations declining. Also, because plants make oxygen and use up carbon dioxide, cutting trees down means more carbon dioxide in the air, which contributes to global warming.

Peat bogs are important for biodiversity and as 'carbon sinks', which means they absorb harmful carbon dioxide. Peat bogs have been dug up for fuel and to make garden compost.

POLLUTION

Pollution is closely linked to climate change, but polluted water, air and soil are also very damaging to wildlife. For example, nutrients from fertilisers cause problems when they run into water sources, killing fish and other living things.

Modern farming often uses monoculture to maximise yield and profit. But this reduces biodiversity and has other negative effects on the environment, such as using more fertilisers and pesticides.

Millions of people rely on fish for food and to sell, but overfishing threatens this. Industries like fishing need to be sustainable to safeguard both biodiversity and future people's livelihoods.

OTHER HUMAN ACTIVITIES

Other threats include exploiting resources faster than they can renew themselves (such as overfishing), illegal poaching, monoculture and disturbing natural environments, for example for tourism and leisure.

MAPPING THE AMAZON RAINFOREST

The Amazon is the most biodiverse place on Earth and is vital for the planet's health in combatting global warming. But this special place is vulnerable – an area of rainforest roughly the size of a football pitch is cut down every single minute.

This false-colour map from NASA shows the diversity of vegetation in the Amazon and the impact of farming.

MAP MASTERS

Despite its importance, the Amazon is difficult to map and study, but improvements in satellites, computing and cartography have made this much easier. False-colour satellite images (like the map shown here) can show changes in things, such as vegetation, more clearly than a photo would.

- Rainforest
- Land cleared for pasture
- Seasonally flooded savanna and other wetlands
- Bare ground
- Desert

FACT

At least 10 per cent of the biodiversity in the entire world can be found here.

The Amazon Rainforest is the world's largest tropical forest, but it has lost 17 per cent of its forest cover over the last 50 years.

1 FOREST TO PASTURE

Cattle pastures have encroached into tropical rainforest here.

2 SAVANNA TO CROPLAND

Large areas of tropical savanna (grassland) in this area are now used to grow crops.

HEALTHY RAINFOREST, HEALTHY PLANET

We need tropical rainforests like the Amazon for a healthy planet. They take carbon dioxide out of the atmosphere, release oxygen and act as vast carbon sinks. Deforestation and burning forests have the opposite effect, releasing more carbon dioxide, which directly contributes to global warming.

AMAZON: SOUTH AMERICA

PROTECTING BIODIVERSITY

There are billions of people on Earth. We need to protect biodiversity for our own survival, as well as that of the millions of species we share the planet with.

CONSERVATION

Put simply, we need to do more of the things that conserve habitats and species, and do less of the things that harm them. This means protecting habitats by creating conservation areas or National Parks, preserving endangered species and bringing them back to areas where they have died out. It also means reducing deforestation and other threats to biodiversity, and tackling climate change.

Captive breeding programmes try to conserve endangered species like the giant panda.

Around 10,000 African rhinos have been killed by poachers for their horns in the last decade. Both white and black rhinos have been rescued, reintroduced and protected in Botswana.

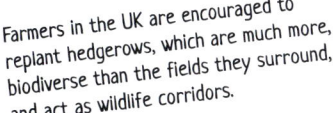

Farmers in the UK are encouraged to replant hedgerows, which are much more biodiverse than the fields they surround, and act as wildlife corridors.

WHO CAN HELP?

Increasingly, the world is realising that high biodiversity is crucial to our future. Biodiversity affects everyone, so it should be everyone's responsibility. We need governments to establish more National Parks and make laws to tackle climate change, but a lot of conservation efforts are thanks to charities and individuals. Everyone can help to conserve species and habitats.

WHAT CAN YOU DO?

If you have a garden, you can help biodiversity by including plants that attract bees and butterflies, making piles of wood and rocks or having a 'wild' corner. You can change your own habits to reduce energy, shop sustainably and recycle rather than sending waste to landfill. You can also volunteer for local charities and put pressure on politicians to make big changes.

What can you do to make changes in your area? Lots of conservation depends on local volunteers.

MAPPING NORTH AMERICA

Bringing just one species back to an ecosystem can have a positive effect on its biodiversity.

KEYSTONE SPECIES

A keystone is the central stone in an arch – without it, the arch collapses. Without what are called 'keystone species', an entire ecosystem can collapse too. Scientists divide keystone species into predators (like otters), engineers (like beavers) and mutualists (things that help each other, like bees pollinating plants).

1 MAKAH BAY

A zoologist came up with the name 'keystone species' in the 1960s after an experiment at Makah Bay. When he removed the top predator, a starfish, a type of mussel took over, leading to a far less diverse ecosystem.

This map looks at keystone species reintroduced to North America.

2 BRITISH COLUMBIA

Kelp (seaweed) forests are important ecosystems that are damaged by too many sea urchins. Sea otters eat sea urchins. Hunted for their fur, the otters had died out in British Columbia, but reintroductions and a hunting ban mean numbers are rising.

3 YELLOWSTONE NATIONAL PARK

Reintroducing wolves, a keystone species, to Yellowstone has had a dramatic effect on the ecosystem. Wolves keep elk on the move, which results in more vegetation and therefore more beavers, another keystone species.

4 COLORADO

Like sea otters, river otters were also hunted, and have suffered from habitat loss and water pollution. However, reintroductions in Colorado and other states have been very successful.

5 SAN PEDRO RIVER

Once so common this was called 'Beaver River', beavers were hunted to extinction here for their furs. Beavers are ecosystem 'engineers' because they build dams, changing the environment in a way that helps other animals. Reintroducing beavers has increased the number and diversity of birds around this river.

GLOSSARY

biodiversity the variety of plant and animal life in an area

carbon dioxide a gas made when things are burned and that people and animals breathe out

climate change the rising temperature of the Earth's surface and its effects, such as melting ice caps and more extreme weather

colonisation when one country takes control of land in another country

deforestation cutting down trees and clearing the land

diversity a range of different things

ecosystem all the living things in an area and how they affect each other and their environment

endemic found only in a particular place

evolution the way living things gradually change over time

genes the parts of living cells that control which characteristics parents pass on to offspring

global warming the rising temperature of the Earth's surface; it is caused by very high levels of carbon dioxide and other greenhouse gases in the atmosphere

herbicide a chemical used to kill or slow the growth of plants such as weeds

migration when birds or animals move to another place, often at certain times of the year

monoculture farming just one type of crop

poaching illegal hunting

pollinate to fertilise a plant

pollution the act of damaging the natural world with harmful substances

reintroduce to bring a species back to an area where it has died out

spawn to lay eggs

species a kind of plant or animal

sustainable describes something that can continue for a long time because it does not harm the environment

FURTHER INFORMATION

Books

Oceans (The Big Picture) by Jon Richards (Franklin Watts, 2020)

Animals at Risk (Fact Planet) by Izzi Howell (Franklin Watts, 2020)

Biodiversity (Ecographics) by Izzi Howell (Franklin Watts, 2019)

Websites

www.amnh.org/explore/ology/biodiversity#all

Find biodiversity games, stories and hands-on projects at this site.

www.bbc.co.uk/bitesize/topics/z3fycdm/articles/zk9cxyc

Find out more about the Galápagos Islands and test yourself with a quiz.

wwf.panda.org/knowledge_hub/where_we_work

The charity WWF works in the most biodiverse places in the world – use the map on this page to click and explore.

INDEX

Amazon Rainforest **24–25**
Australia **20–21**

biodiversity hotspots **5**

climate change **4, 8, 15, 22, 23, 26, 27**
conservation **26–27**
coral reefs **8, 17**
Coral Triangle **8–9**

Darwin, Charles **10, 12, 13**
deforestation **17, 22, 25, 26**

ecosystems **4, 6, 7, 14–15, 16, 18, 28, 29**
evolution **10, 11, 12, 13, 16**
extinction **7, 11, 13, 16, 22, 29**

farming **22, 23, 24, 25, 27**
fishing **8, 9, 23**
food **4, 6, 7, 8, 21**
food chains and webs **14, 15**

Galápagos Islands **12–13**
global warming **22, 24, 25**

habitat loss **4, 5, 15, 17, 22, 29**
habitats **4, 18, 20, 26, 27**
health **4, 6, 7**

invasive species **18–21, 22**
islands **12–13, 16, 19**

keystone species **28, 29**

Madagascar **16–17**

North America **28–29**

poaching **23, 26**
pollution **4, 5, 23, 29**

rainforests **4, 7, 16, 24–25**
reintroducing species **26, 28–29**

tourism **5, 8, 23**

TITLES IN THE MAP YOUR PLANET SERIES

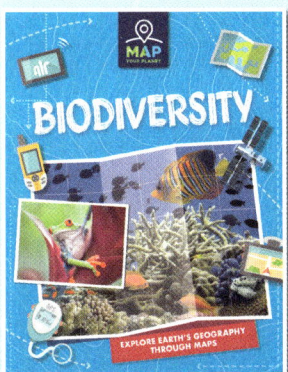

What is biodiversity?
Why do we need biodiversity?
Mapping the Coral Triangle
Evolution and extinction
Mapping the Galápagos Islands
Ecosystems
Mapping Madagascar
Invasive species
Mapping Australia
Biodiversity under threat
Mapping the Amazon Rainforest
Protecting biodiversity
Mapping North America

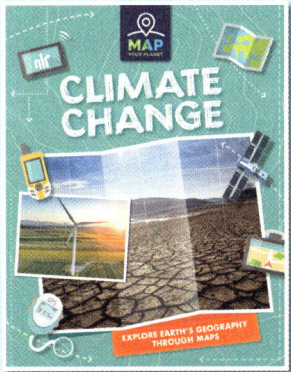

What is climate change?
What causes climate change?
Mapping CO_2 emissions
Melting ice
Mapping the Arctic
The oceans
Mapping Bangladesh
Extreme weather
Mapping Europe
The natural world
Mapping the Great Barrier Reef
The future
Mapping a greener world

What is a habitat?
Types of habitat
Mapping global biomes
Tundra
Mapping northern Russia
Forests
Mapping the Americas
Grasslands
Mapping the Serengeti
Deserts
Mapping the Sahara
Water habitats
Mapping the Mekong River

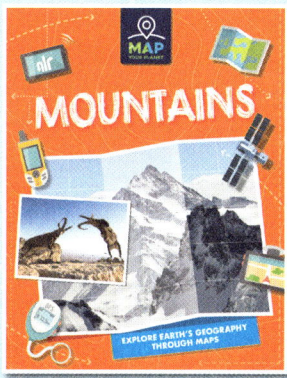

What are mountains?
Shifting Earth
Mapping the Ring of Fire
Fold mountains
Mapping the Himalayas
Faults and domes
Mapping the Sierra Nevada
On the plateau
Mapping New Zealand's volcanic plateau
Volcanic mountains
Mapping the Hawaiian Islands
People in the mountains
Mapping the Alps

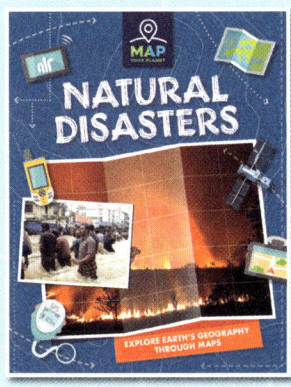

What is a natural disaster?
Volcanoes
Mapping Vesuvius
Earthquakes and tsunamis
Mapping the 2004 Indian Ocean tsunami
Extreme weather
Mapping Haiti
Floods
Mapping East Africa
Droughts
Mapping south-eastern Australia
People and natural disasters
Mapping climate disasters

Earth's resources
A world of water
Mapping the Ganges River
Living off the land
Mapping the Netherlands
Woodland wonderland
Mapping Finland's forests
Mineral mining
Mapping Bingham Canyon mine
Fossil fuels
Mapping the Middle East oil fields
Clean resources
Mapping the Itaipú Dam

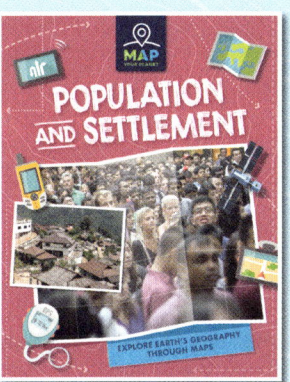

Population and settlement
Distribution and density
Mapping global population
Population growth
Mapping Niger and Japan
Migration
Mapping US immigration
Early settlements
Mapping Tenochtitlan
Settlement types and patterns
Mapping London
Changing settlements
Mapping Shanghai

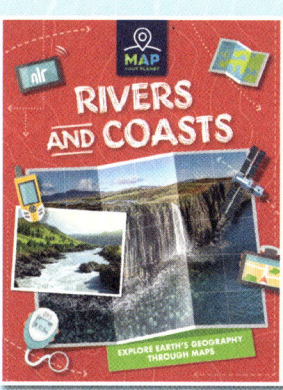

Rivers and coasts
A river's source
Mapping the Amazon River
The upper and middle courses
Mapping the Kentucky Bend
Reaching the sea
Mapping the Nile Delta
Types of coast
Mapping new shores
Coastal changes
Mapping La Manga
Using water
Mapping the Three Gorges Dam